D0487801

30128 80270 993 0

DESTINATION:
SPACE

WIDE EYED EDITIONS

Destination: The Beginning of Time

Are you ready to go on the most exciting adventure in the universe? Welcome on board! Together we are going to travel through space to the edges of the Milky Way and beyond, see Earth as you've never seen it before, escape a black hole, see a star being born, and more. First, our journey takes us to the dawn of time...

Our universe is almost 14 billion years old. That means, if you counted one grain of sand for each of these years, you could fill an entire lorry with sand.

But how did it all begin? To find out, you have to look billions of years into the past, to the very origins of the universe.

At the beginning there was the Big Bang, which was the birth of space and time. Although the Big Bang happened so long ago, we can still see its echo in the sky – not with our bare eyes, but with satellite telescopes we have sent into space that can detect heat traces of the early universe.

The Big Bang

When the BIG BANG happened, everything was much hotter than anything we can see in the universe today.

Look outside — nothing structured, such as planets or galaxies existed. It was so hot that matter, as we detect it today, did not exist, there was just a SOUP OF PARTICLES.

At that time, the HOT TEMPERATURE made elementary particles jiggle so hard that they could not bind together to form ATOMS.

The Universe Expands

We're not certain what happened during the tiniest fractions of a second after the Big Bang, but we think the universe GREW EXTREMELY FAST. Everything happened really quickly!

To think of how space and time grew, imagine a balloon inflating at a speed faster than the speed of light. As the universe grew, it COOLED DOWN.

The universe got colder because its heat was spread out across the increasing space. This all happened in a moment billions of times shorter than a single second — and the universe did not stop expanding... it just SLOWED DOWN. And the more it expanded, the colder the universe became.

0 secs   0.01 secs   3 mins

Timeline of Events

Although the Big Bang was very sudden, the Universe took much longer to form its present shape.

Around three minutes after the Big Bang, the first NUCLEI formed.

Four hundred thousand years after Big Bang, the FIRST ATOMS appeared.

600 million years after the Big Bang, the first STARS similar to our own star, the Sun, were born.

electron

proton neutron

Atom

Atoms Form

Just one second after the Big Bang, the universe had cooled enough for the first elementary particles to stop jiggling and bind together to form particles called PROTONS and NEUTRONS.

Much later, protons and neutrons bound together again forming the cores of atoms, called NUCLEI. Atoms are the building blocks of matter that surrounds us today. Everything in the universe is made out of ATOMS — even you and me!

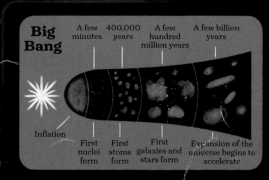

Big Bang

A few minutes | 400,000 years | A few hundred million years | A few billion years

Inflation

First nuclei form | First atoms form | First galaxies and stars form | Expansion of the universe begins to accelerate

The Universe Today

If you look into the night sky, you can see the light of the galaxy that we belong to. It is called the Milky Way and it's made up of billions of stars and planets.

The Milky Way is not the only galaxy in the universe – in fact, most of the distant lights you see at night are actually whole galaxies!

All the material in the universe that we can see – from huge stars, to clouds of dust (and even us humans!) – is called 'matter'. When you look into space, it might seem as if there is an overwhelming amount of this stuff, but in fact, this isn't true – matter makes up less than five per cent of the universe.

The two other substances which make up the rest of the 95 per cent are much more common, but are much harder to find and observe...

Dark Matter

More than a quarter of the universe is made up of dark matter. Our instruments can't detect it properly because it interacts with them far more weakly than normal matter, and this is why scientists have called it 'dark matter' – because it SEEMS INVISIBLE to us.

Although we can't see dark matter, or even detect it with scientific experiments, we know it has to be there! We WATCH HOW GALAXIES MOVE, and the only way to explain the way they behave is to assume that some extra stuff must be there, even though we can't see it.

The Universe

Dark energy: 68.3%

Dark matter: 26.8%

Matter: 4.9%

Compared to MATTER, which we can detect, how much dark energy and dark matter is there in the universe?

Dark Energy

Scientists think the rest of the universe is made up of dark energy, which is completely different to normal matter — or dark matter! Scientists are still UNSURE WHAT DARK ENERGY IS exactly, but they are certain that it exists.

They think dark energy is more like a property of the universe, and that this is the reason why the universe is still EXPANDING today.

Gravity

We all know gravity as the force that pulls us – and other things – to the ground.

The legend goes that an apple falling on Isaac Newton's head inspired him to write the first theory of gravity in 1687. His theory states that all things made of matter are attracted to each other: the Earth attracted the apple, making it fall to the ground. In the same way, the Earth attracts us, pulling us down and keeping us from floating into space.

But Newton's theory also means that the Earth would have been attracted in return by the apple. However, we can't really see this happening because the Earth is much bigger than an apple, and its pull is much stronger.

However, in space there are much bigger objects – like planets, stars and moons – and this is where you can see the effect of gravity between two objects.

The Moon

Earth's gravity keeps the Moon MOVING AROUND EARTH, and stops it flying off into space.

And we can feel the Moon's gravity on Earth, too. It pulls the water in our oceans, and this causes the TIDES to rise and fall.

High tide

Low tide

Earth's tides

High tide

Gravity

Moon - - - - - - - Earth

Low tide

Weightlessness

When you are in space, you feel weightless. This is because you do not feel the effect of EARTH'S GRAVITY anymore.

The Sun

The Sun is so much bigger than the Earth or the Moon that its gravity attracts our Earth, making the Earth orbit the Sun in the same way that the Moon moves around the Earth. The Sun's gravity also keeps all the other planets in our SOLAR SYSTEM IN ORBIT.

Pioneers of Gravity

>> Johannes Kepler   >> Isaac Newton

Gravity wasn't all Newton's idea. We mustn't forget JOHANNES KEPLER! This German astronomer investigated the motion of the planets in our Solar System, and thanks to him we understood the motion of planets before Newton.

But it was NEWTON'S THEORY that showed the reason for the planets' motion was gravity. And without Kepler and Newton's work all those years ago, we wouldn't be able to travel in space today.

Einstein's Theory

ALBERT EINSTEIN took this theory to the next level! He explained gravity in terms of space and time, like this: if you hold a sheet and put a weight in the middle, the sheet bends and curves. Now when you roll a marble over the sheet, its path will follow the bends in the sheet, and it looks like as if the marble is attracted to the weight. The piece of fabric represents space and time in Einstein's theory.

Einstein predicted that everything that moves in space feels gravity, EVEN LIGHT. This was an entirely new idea. Shortly after Einstein predicted that light would bend around big masses, a team of astronomers did indeed observe light bending around the Sun. This showed that Einstein's theory was correct and it is still the best theory of gravity we have today.

Where the star actually is

Where the star appears to be

Light

Sun

Earth

Galaxies

A galaxy is a collection of stars and planets, held together by gravity.

We are part of a galaxy called the Milky Way, and as well as stars and planets, it also contains lots of interstellar dust and gas, and mysterious dark matter.

Scientists have estimated there are more than 100 billion galaxies in our universe. They have to use telescopes to observe them because most of these galaxies can't be seen with the naked eye.

Kinds of Galaxy

Scientists have found galaxies of VARIOUS SHAPES AND SIZES — small dwarf galaxies, and others a thousand times bigger than our Milky Way. Some have structure, like spiral arms, while others can appear as just a cloud of stars.

| Spiral | Elliptical | Irregular |

Andromeda

The closest big galaxy to the Milky Way is called Andromeda and it is similar to us in shape and size. But even though it is our CLOSEST NEIGHBOUR, it is still so far away that light takes 2.5 million years to travel through space to reach us!

Like everything else in the universe, the Milky Way and Andromeda are ATTRACTED BY GRAVITY. This causes them to slowly drift towards each other through space. In the very distant future they will merge together to form an even bigger galaxy!

Milky Way   Andromeda

Hubble Telescope

Using the Hubble Space Telescope, scientists searched a tiny patch of the sky to look for the galaxies very far away from us. In this small region — which is smaller than a millionth of the size of the entire sky — they found THOUSANDS OF GALAXIES.

Those are the most distant galaxies we know of today. The light from those galaxies takes over TEN BILLION YEARS to reach us. So we see them today as they were a long time ago... Which means that we are actually looking back in time! Because these are the most distant galaxies, they are also the oldest we know of.

They are the EARLIEST GALAXIES that formed after the Big Bang, and because the light takes so long to travel to us, we see them as they were when they were very young and just started to appear. Looking back in time like this gives scientists a lot of information on how galaxies, and everything they contain, began.

The Milky Way

The Milky Way is the galaxy our Sun and our Solar System are part of.

You can see our Milky Way as a glowing band in the night sky. As well as our Sun, scientists think it contains around 100 billion other stars, many of them with planetary systems like our own Solar System.

The Milky Way is a spiral galaxy. It looks like a disc with four big spiral arms. It is so big that it takes more than one hundred thousand years for light to travel from one end of the galaxy to the other.

The Milky Way from Earth

How Old is the Milky Way?

The Milky Way is very old, almost as old as the universe itself. Astronomers estimate the age of the oldest stars in the Milky Way to be around 12 BILLION YEARS OLD, meaning that those stars formed comparatively soon after the birth of the universe.

The Shape of the Milky Way

Perseus Arm

Outer Arm

Sagittarius A

Our Sun

Sagittarius
Carina Arm

Where is our Solar System?

Our Solar System is 27,000 LIGHT YEARS away from the centre of the Milky Way outside the disc part.

What's at the Centre?

At the centre of the Milky Way, there is a SUPERMASSIVE BLACK HOLE in an area called Sagittarius A*. Radio signals from this black hole take 27,000 years to reach us.

Our Solar System

Satellite Galaxies

The Milky Way is so big that it has several SMALLER GALAXIES ORBITING IT, in the same way the Earth has the Moon and other satellites travelling around it.

This is why astronomers refer to such galaxies as Milky Way's 'satellite galaxies'. The biggest one of these is the MAGELLANIC CLOUD, which is ten times smaller than our Milky Way.

Stars

In the night sky, a star might look like a tiny pinprick of light, but up close, you'll discover it is a massive ball of hot, burning gas.

One star that you will already know is the Sun. The Sun isn't the biggest star in the sky, but it is the closest star to us, which is why it looks so much larger and brighter than the others we can see at night.

Each star in our night sky began life as a cloud of swirling gas, left over from the Big Bang, or an old, exploded star. Over time, gravity caused this cloudy mass to group together and spin into a ball of hot, dense gas. Eventually, the ball formed a star. New stars are still in the process of being born all over the universe.

A STAR BEGINS as a massive cloud of gas and dust. The hydrogen and helium gases react with each other, causing the cloud to collapse in on itself, and from this swirling cloud, a star is born.

The Life Cycle of a Star

At the end of its life, an average star will grow a lot bigger in size. As it grows, its surface cools, which causes it to CHANGE COLOUR from yellow-white (like the Sun) to red.

We talk about these stars as RED GIANTS. Our own Sun will develop into a red giant, but not for another 5 billion years. By then, it will have grown so big that its surface will reach the orbit of the Earth!

Average star

Red giant

Interstellar cloud

Massive star

Red supergiant

Young stars that are more than eight times bigger than our Sun are called MASSIVE STARS, and others, which are more than fifty times the size, are called SUPERMASSIVE STARS.

As nuclear fusion causes a massive star to swell, it becomes a RED SUPERGIANT. These stars are the biggest in the universe, but they are not very dense.

Nuclear Fusion

Stars are fuelled by a reaction that takes place inside them called nuclear fusion, which releases a lot of energy in the form of LIGHT AND HEAT.

The light and heat from our star, the Sun, keeps Earth warm enough to make LIFE here possible.

When a star begins to RUN OUT OF FUEL, there is nothing to stop it from collapsing in under its own gravity.

Stars like our Sun will eventually develop into a WHITE DWARF.

Planetary nebula

White dwarf

...Or sometimes, a supernova can create a NEUTRON STAR, which is very exotic! It is small in size — only 30 kilometres across — but very dense.

It is so dense that normal atoms do not form and the entire planet is composed of NEUTRONS — the tiniest inner part of an atom.

Neutron star

Black hole

After a supernova explosion, the remnants can form a BLACK HOLE...

Supernova

A massive explosion like a supernova might seem like a very destructive event, but from this blast come HEAVY ATOMS that you can find inside the human body... We humans truly come from the stars!

Stars that are ten times heavier than our Sun can EXPLODE IN A SUPERNOVA. This kind of explosion is so violent and bright that it can outshine entire galaxies in the sky for days!

Black Holes

Scientists think that most galaxies hide an invisible secret at their centre...

Something with such a strong gravitational pull that even huge stars and entire Solar Systems feel its effect. They think this force comes from a black hole.

But what is a black hole? This is a region of space where gravity is so strong that nothing can escape from it, not even light.

Is information lost forever inside a black hole? Black holes are the ultimate test of our understanding of gravity itself, but scientists think that answering questions like these will help us find a new and better theory of gravity.

Event Horizon

A black hole is surrounded by an invisible boundary called an event horizon. You can think of the event horizon like the edge of a waterfall — beyond this point gravity becomes too strong and everything that passes this boundary is sucked inside the black hole.

Spaghettification

Scientists think that objects change shape and are stretched long and thin as they are sucked into a black hole. This is called spaghettification, or the NOODLE EFFECT.

Observing Black Holes

How do we know a black hole is there if we can't see it?'

Using telescopes, we can watch stars close to a black hole, and calculate its location from their paths as they travel through space.

If stars happen to be too close to a black hole, we can even observe matter being sucked away from that star towards the black hole.

How Are Black Holes Made?

The heavier an object is, the stronger its GRAVITATIONAL FORCE. If you stand on a big planet, you will feel a strong force of gravity... And massive stars have a massive gravitational force!

Now remember, gravity affects everything, not just people and objects. That means the SURFACE OF THE EARTH itself feels the gravity of its own core and is pulled inwards towards it.

Gravity pulls Earth's surface inwards

Earth

Resistant force pushes back

But instead of falling inwards, like water down a plughole, the Earth's surface is stopped from crushing in on itself by a RESISTANT FORCE – the same force that makes the ground resist your foot and allows you to walk.

However, if a star is heavy enough, the resistant force that keeps its surface from falling inwards might not be strong enough to balance the star's gravity at the end of its lifetime. If that is the case, the star will start to SHRINK.

As the star continues to shrink, more and more of its matter becomes COMPRESSED at its centre, making the gravitational attraction of its core even bigger...

Massive star

Resistant force is weaker than pull of star's gravity

Once this starts to happen, nothing can stop the star from collapsing to its centre. It forms a BLACK HOLE.

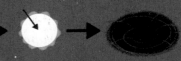

Star collapses

Black hole forms

The Sun

The Sun is the star at the centre of our Solar System, and the source of Earth's light and energy.

It is 1.3 million times bigger than the Earth, and a lot hotter – about 5,500 degrees Celsius on its surface! – with hot gas that surrounds it in a halo, which extends millions of kilometres into space.

This atmosphere of gases around the Sun is called the corona, and it can be seen from Earth with special telescopes. You can also see the corona during a solar eclipse, when it appears like a golden ring around the Moon.

Light

It's only when the light gets a long way away from the core that the Sun's density becomes low enough for the light to ESCAPE.

The Sun's Energy

The Sun is heated by nuclear fusion. Inside its core, hydrogen is continuously melted together to form helium, which releases Energy.

This is the part of the Sun that we can see on Earth — scientists call it the PHOTOSPHERE.

Further away from the Sun's core, this energy is converted to LIGHT... But the Sun is so dense that this light cannot escape!

Sun Spots

The Sun's surface is not equally hot all over, and there are small areas that are cooler, which appear as BLACK SPOTS...

...These are called SUNSPOTS, and although they might look small, they can be 50,000 kilometres across. They are very active areas on the Sun's surface and explosions — called solar flares — erupt from them.

Solar Wind

It's not only light and heat that are emitted from the photosphere, but streams of MAGNETICALLY CHARGED PARTICLES, called solar wind, too. This can create all kinds of problems...

...It can cause satellites to break down, radio blackouts, and do damage to spacecraft. But solar wind also creates the amazing light displays at the north and south poles, called AURORA BOREALIS (in the north) and AURORA AUSTRALIS (in the south).

Aurora

Solar wind

Magnetic shield   Magnetic field

The Solar System

Eight planets, including Earth, orbit the Sun, making up our Solar System.

The Solar System covers a vast region of space. You would need to spend around 22,000 years driving on the motorway to travel from the Sun to the outer edges of the Solar System... And light travels this distance in just under 20 minutes!

Neptune

Earth

Mars

Uranus

Mercury

Saturn

Venus

Jupiter

The SUN is the centre of the Solar System. Everything in the Solar System travels around the Sun in circular paths.

A planet's journey around the Sun is known as its 'ORBIT'. Usually the shape of the path is a stretched circle, called an ellipse.

Mercury

The planet closest to the Sun is MERCURY. It's located about halfway between the Sun and the Earth. Its surface is covered with big craters, just like the Moon.

Mercury is the SMALLEST PLANET in the Solar System — almost twenty times smaller than Earth. It is too small to have an atmosphere to protect it from meteoroids, which is why it's covered with craters.

Venus

The second-closest planet to the Sun is VENUS. It's about the same size as Earth, but the conditions there are quite different! Its atmosphere is so dense that we cannot see its surface from space.

Earth

Doesn't it look awesome from space? We'll be turning back to look at this in a bit more detail later on.

Look at EARTH!

Mars

Our fourth planet is MARS.

Mars is almost seven times smaller than Earth, making it the SECOND SMALLEST planet in the Solar System after Mercury.

It's easy to spot from Earth because of its distinctive RED GLOW.

Jupiter

Next comes JUPITER, the fifth — and biggest — planet in our Solar System.

It is called a GAS GIANT, because it has a rock core surrounded by liquid hydrogen and a lot of gas.

Its eye-catching great RED SPOT is a massive storm — two to three times the size of the Earth — that has been raging for more than 300 years.

Saturn

Then comes SATURN.

Saturn looks the most distinctive amongst all planets in the Solar System: it is surrounded by RINGS OF ICE! Astronomers think these rings might once have been part of one of Saturn's MOONS.

It is ten times further away from the Sun than Earth. It is also a GAS GIANT, but it is not quite as big as Jupiter.

Uranus

We're at the outer reaches now, passing by URANUS.

This is another gas giant — and it's 60 TIMES BIGGER than the Earth.

Neptune

Finally, the last planet in the Solar System is Neptune. It is another gas giant — but that's not everything!

Between Mars and Jupiter there is a wide belt of asteroids, and beyond Neptune is PLUTO, almost a thousand times smaller than the Earth, and therefore a dwarf planet. And after Pluto, we'll find the Kuiper belt, another belt of asteroids. Beyond this, we approach the edges of our Solar System, which is where INTERSTELLAR SPACE begins... And our adventures continue!

Light

What is light? This is a question that has puzzled physicists for a very long time.

James Clerk Maxwell was a Scottish physicist alive in the 19th century, who studied electric and magnetic effects. While he worked on his theory, (which talked about electric currents, and that magnets have a north and south pole) his calculations also – unexpectedly – predicted that there should be waves travelling through space, just as ripples travel across the water's surface when you drop a stone in a pond.

Maxwell quickly realised that these waves were predicted to travel at the speed of light. This forced him to conclude that light is, in fact, an electromagnetic wave.

Frequency

Electromagnetic waves have different properties, depending on their frequency. 'Frequency' describes the NUMBER OF RIPPLES that appear each second. The frequency is HIGH if there are lots of ripples with a short wavelength. The frequency is LOW if there are fewer ripples, with a long wavelength.

Frequency (Hz)

Wavelength (m)

Radio: 50m

Microwave: 0.1m

Football pitch

Butterfly

Electromagnetic Spectrum

The light we see with our naked eye, however, is just a small range of all the frequencies there actually can be. The entire range of frequencies of light is called the electromagnetic spectrum. We use parts of this spectrum in our DAILY LIFE.

For instance, rays with a SMALLER FREQUENCY than red light are used in microwave ovens, or to transmit radio and television signals.

Rays with a HIGHER FREQUENCY than blue light are used in x-ray machines to take pictures of the bones inside our bodies.

Visible Light

With light that we can see with our eyes, the higher and lower frequencies appear as different COLOURS.

RED LIGHT has a lower frequency (with a longer wavelength), while BLUE LIGHT has a higher frequency (with a shorter wavelength).

Infrared: 10^{-4}m

Visible light: 10^{-6}m

Ultraviolet rays: 10^{-8}m

X-rays: 10^{-10}m

Gamma rays: 10^{-12}m

Needle head

Bacterium

Virus

Atom

Atomic nucleus

What is the width of each wavelength equivalent to?

Photons

In the early 1900s, physicists found out that describing light as a wave could not be entirely true. Albert Einstein proposed that we should think about light also as a collection of particles of light called photons. Using this idea, physicists have since developed a theory called QUANTUM MECHANICS that tells us how photons behave.

Through understanding quantum mechanics, we have learnt how to build COMPUTERS and LASERS. Modern life would not be possible without our discoveries about light.

Earth and its Magnetic Field

Earth is the densest planet in the entire Solar System, which means that it is the heaviest planet compared to its size.

Like other planets made of rock, such as Mars, Earth is made up of different layers like an onion. Its outer core is mostly made up of melted iron, and, as the Earth spins, the molten metal moves around. This creates electrical currents in the inner core, turning the metal there into a kind of giant magnet.

Because of this, Earth has a huge magnetic field that extends out into space. This magnetic field gives Earth its North and South Poles. It also acts like an invisible shield, which protects Earth from harmful particles that would damage our atmosphere.

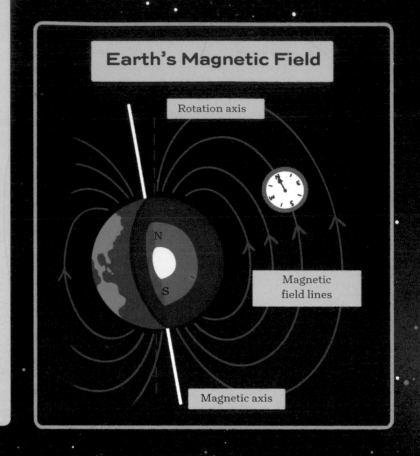

Earth's Magnetic Field

Rotation axis

N

S

Magnetic field lines

Magnetic axis

Northern Lights

Near to the Earth's poles, you can sometimes see a spectacular LIGHT DISPLAY in the sky.

Up in the North Pole it is called the Aurora Borealis, and down in the South Pole it is called the Aurora Australis. This is caused by SOLAR WIND which comes from the Sun.

As the solar wind particles hit Earth's ATMOSPHERE, they collide with the oxygen and nitrogen particles, making them glow green, blue or red.

Earth's Cycles

Not only does the Earth travel around the Sun, but it also spins around itself.

When we talk about a 'day', in scientific terms, we mean the time that the Earth takes to spin around on itself one single time. This takes 24 hours, during which time we experience night and day.

Look at the land ahead of us – it's bright daylight at midday. As the day progresses, Earth will continue to spin, moving this land away from the Sun, causing the Sun to set there.

Behind us you can see the parts of Earth where it is night time. This is because the Sun's rays are blocked there. But as the Earth keeps spinning, this part of Earth will turn towards the Sun. The Sun will rise, bringing morning, then midday... and finally night, when everything starts over again!

SUMMER in the Northern Hemisphere: Earth is tilted towards the Sun.

Spring in the Northern Hemisphere

WINTER in the Northern Hemisphere: Earth is tilted away from the Sun.

Sun

WINTER in the Southern Hemisphere: Earth is tilted away from the Sun.

Autumn in the Northern Hemisphere

SUMMER in the Southern Hemisphere: Earth is tilted towards the Sun.

Earth's Seasons

As Earth orbits the Sun, it spins on a TILTED AXIS. This means that the parts above and below the equator receive different amounts of sunshine.

This causes the four SEASONS – spring, summer, autumn and winter.

When the NORTHERN HEMISPHERE is tilted towards the Sun, it receives more sunlight and it becomes summer there – the days are long and it can get quite hot!

At the same time, the SOUTHERN HEMISPHERE is tilted away from the Sun and receives less sunlight. The people there experience WINTER with shorter days, longer nights and cooler temperatures.

A Year on Earth

It takes Earth 365 ¼ days to complete an orbit of the Sun. We call this a YEAR. Every four years we have a leap year: we add the four quarter days up and give the month of February an extra day.

Earth's Atmosphere

The atmosphere of the Earth is the air that surrounds it, and it is made up of different layers.

This thin layer of gas is what protects us from space, and the electromagnetic radiation given off by stars like the Sun. It is because of the atmosphere that life on Earth is possible – without it, we'd have no air to breathe, and would be fried by electromagnetic rays!

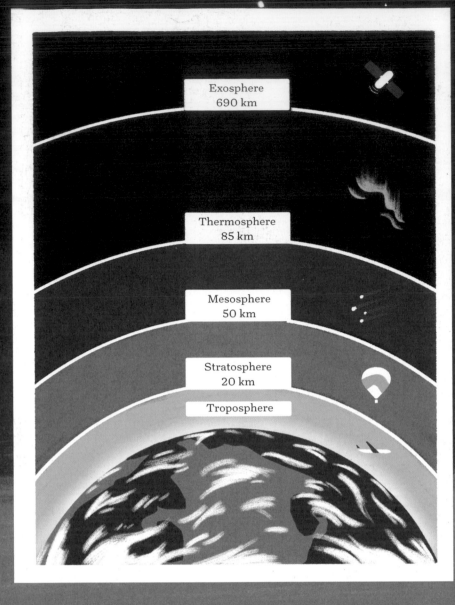

Exosphere
690 km

Thermosphere
85 km

Mesosphere
50 km

Stratosphere
20 km

Troposphere

Stratosphere

Here is where you'll find the OZONE LAYER. Ozone is a special type of oxygen that reacts with very energetic sunlight and releases heat. Because of this, as you travel through the stratosphere, the higher you climb, the warmer it gets!

The ozone layer is very important for life on Earth — it acts as a shield against HARMFUL RAYS that would cause disease, and heat Earth up to the point where life would become impossible.

Troposphere

This layer directly SURROUNDS US, and is mostly heated by the Earth, not the Sun's light. This is why, when you travel away from the surface of the Earth, the air temperature becomes colder (about 1°C for every hundred metres you climb).

As the temperature reduces, the air pressure decreases too. AIR PRESSURE is created by the weight of all the air above us. And the further you climb, the less air is above you, and so the lower the air pressure is! When this happens, we say that the air is 'getting thin'.

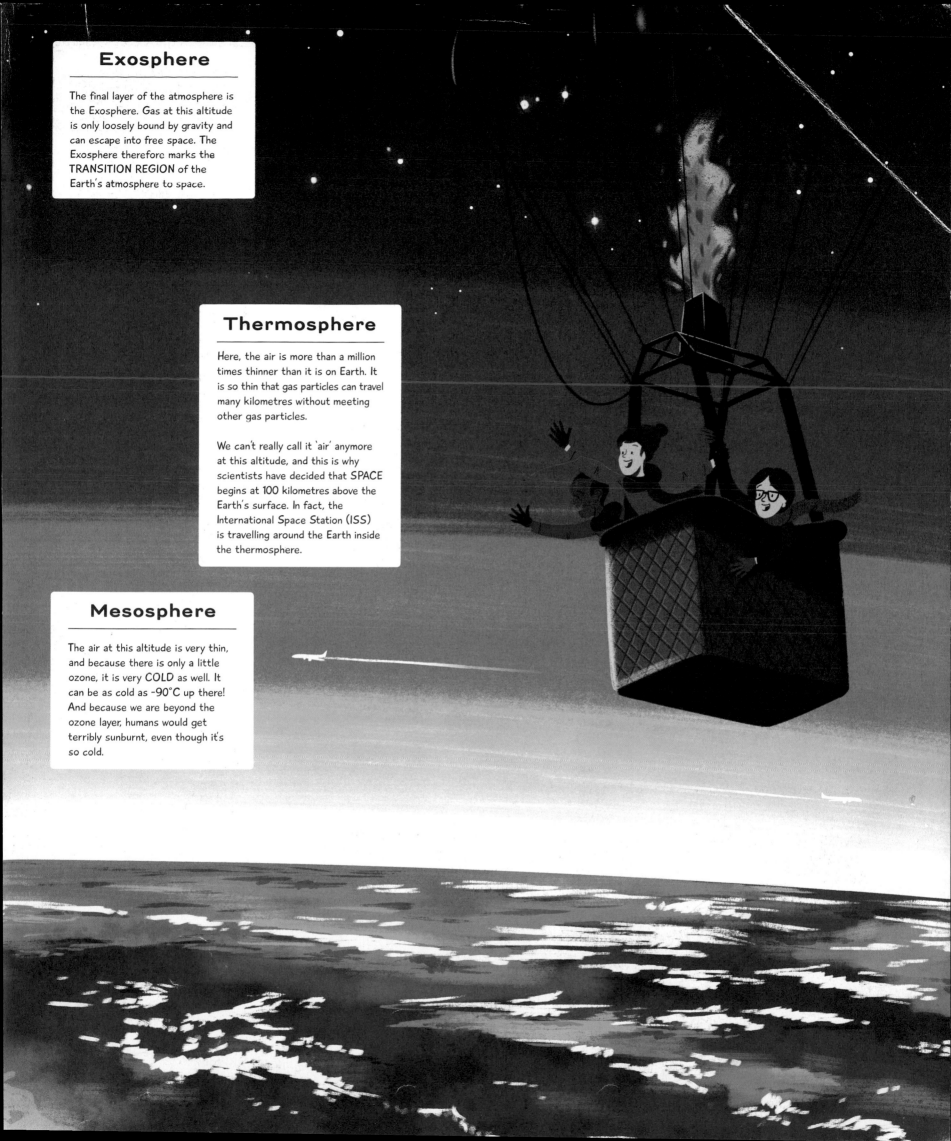

Exosphere

The final layer of the atmosphere is the Exosphere. Gas at this altitude is only loosely bound by gravity and can escape into free space. The Exosphere therefore marks the **TRANSITION REGION** of the Earth's atmosphere to space.

Thermosphere

Here, the air is more than a million times thinner than it is on Earth. It is so thin that gas particles can travel many kilometres without meeting other gas particles.

We can't really call it 'air' anymore at this altitude, and this is why scientists have decided that **SPACE** begins at 100 kilometres above the Earth's surface. In fact, the International Space Station (ISS) is travelling around the Earth inside the thermosphere.

Mesosphere

The air at this altitude is very thin, and because there is only a little ozone, it is very **COLD** as well. It can be as cold as -90°C up there! And because we are beyond the ozone layer, humans would get terribly sunburnt, even though it's so cold.

The Moon

The Moon is four times smaller than the Earth, and a hundred times lighter!

Because of this, gravity makes the Moon travel around the Earth, just like a satellite. It is too light to have an atmosphere, and therefore isn't protected from showers of meteoroids, which is why its surface is covered with craters.

Scientists are still talking about the origin of the Moon. One possible explanation is that it was born when a very young Earth was hit by an object the size of Mars 4.5 billion years ago. This impact produced a lot of debris around Earth, which was eventually bound by gravity and formed into the Moon.

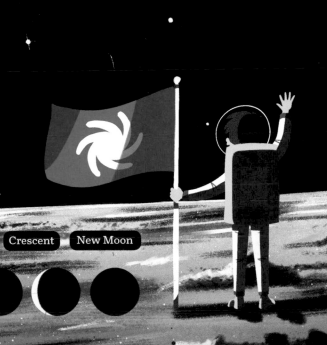

| New Moon | Crescent | Waxing | Full Moon | Waning | Crescent | New Moon |

Moon Phases

It takes around four weeks for the Moon to complete its journey around the Earth. In fact, this is where the word 'MONTH' comes from. During this time, the Moon appears to change because of the way it is lit by the Sun. These changes in its appearance are known as 'PHASES'.

In the Northern Hemisphere, when the Moon is in between the Earth and the Sun, it is called a 'NEW MOON'. During this time, it looks dimmer, because the side of the Moon facing Earth does not receive a lot of sunlight.

Over the next few days, a thin slice becomes visible, which we call a 'CRESCENT MOON'.

This crescent continues to grow in size (when this happens, we say the Moon is 'WAXING') until it is fully illuminated and becomes a 'FULL MOON'.

Then the opposite starts to happen: the Moon begins to shrink in size (we say the Moon is 'WANING') until finally it becomes a 'NEW MOON'.

Journey to the Moon

The Moon has always fascinated people living on Earth, but it was not until 1969 that humans created the technology to leave Earth and make the 384,400 KILOMETRE JOURNEY there.

Neil Armstrong, Michael Collins and Buzz Aldrin were the astronauts on the APOLLO 11 mission that took them to the Moon and safely back to Earth. Neil Armstrong and Buzz Aldrin were the first two humans to set foot on the Moon.

Solar Eclipse

Occasionally, the position of the Moon, the Earth and the Sun mean that a part of the Earth is put in the MOON'S SHADOW. This is called a 'solar eclipse'.

In one particular region on Earth, the SUN'S LIGHT IS BLOCKED by the Moon and it becomes dark in the middle of the day for a few minutes, until the Moon continues in its journey and allows the Sun to shine there again.

Lunar Eclipse

Sometimes, the opposite can happen: the Moon hides in the EARTH'S SHADOW and seems to vanish. This is called a lunar eclipse.

Asteroids, Comets and Meteoroids

Asteroids, comets and meteoroids are smaller objects that are found in our Solar System.

They are too small to be called planets, but behave in a similar way, orbiting in a circular pattern around the Sun. We give these objects different names, depending on their size and properties.

Meteoroids

Meteoroids are much SMALLER VERSIONS OF ASTEROIDS ranging in size from just a few millimetres up to several metres across. Some meteoroids encounter Earth's atmosphere as they travel around the Sun...

Meteors

...And when this happens, the meteoroid turns into a meteor! As the meteoroid enters Earth's atmosphere, it gets so hot that it starts to burn, and develops a SHINING TAIL OF GAS. You can tell what material the meteor is made of from the colour of its tail.

Meteorites

Some meteors survive entering Earth's atmosphere and the impact as it hits the ground. These rocks from space are called meteorites. The largest one is the Hoba Meteorite, which was discovered in Namibia in Africa. It is almost 3 metres long and weighs more than 60 tonnes!

Asteroids

Asteroids come in various shapes and sizes. They aren't round like planets, and look more like big potatoes... Sometimes HUNDREDS OF KILOMETRES ACROSS!

We know of nearly 700,000 asteroids in our Solar System, but there are probably a lot more, and we simply haven't discovered all of them yet.

Comets

Comets are icy rocks and they have a tail similar to a meteor. However, the tail does not emerge because it is entering Earth's atmosphere — instead, when the comet passes close to the Sun on its orbit, the Sun heats the comet up and gas evaporates from it, leaving a trail, which can be observed from Earth. The glow of a comet, however, lasts much longer — a meteor only appears for fractions of a second, while we can observe a comet for days.

Deep Impact

When very big objects like comets or asteroids hit Earth, they can have devastating consequences. Scientists believe that 65 million years ago, the impact of a 15-kilometre-wide asteroid led to the extinction of the dinosaurs! Enormous collisions like this are very unlikely though,

Observing Space From Earth

Humans have always been fascinated by space and the stars, and we have been developing telescopes to better observe space from Earth over hundreds of years.

Today we have telescopes that allow us to see beyond the range of light that we can detect with our naked eyes, by catching ultraviolet and infrared light from stars. This gives scientists the opportunity to study aspects of stars which are hidden from our plain sight.

Early Telescopes

The first telescope was developed in the early 1600s, and used two lenses to magnify the Moon, other planets in the solar system, and the Sun.

While these early telescopes were rather simple compared with our modern instruments, they fuelled our fascination with space.

Modern Te[lescope]

Modern telescopes are much m[ore]
size of a house, with mirrors wh[ich]

The "Very Large Telescope" —
telescopes so far — is made up
To have a clear view, it is locate[d]
mountain in the Atacama Desert in Chile. It can detect light
that is 4 billion times fainter than what a human can observe
with the naked eye, and can even take a picture of a person
standing on the Moon!

pace Travel

Rocket science is the key technology that finally allowed humans to leave Earth.

Space had fascinated humanity for hundreds of years, but it was not until the mid-nineteenth century that space exploration and space travel were finally possible thanks to the development of this new technology.

Only rockets can accelerate spacecrafts to a speed that is high enough to overcome Earth's gravity. This 'escape velocity' is very fast – 10 kilometres per second! At this speed, you could cross the English Channel in just over 3 seconds!

Sputnik

In 1957, the Soviet Union (today called Russia) used a rocket to send Sputnik, the first ARTIFICIAL SATELLITE, to orbit Earth. To calculate Sputnik's orbit, scientists needed to use the biggest supercomputers in the Soviet Union at that time.

Using on-board batteries, Sputnik measured the TEMPERATURE inside and outside the capsule, and sent this information back to Earth. After three weeks, the batteries ran out, and the satellite became inactive. However, Sputnik kept ORBITING EARTH, until it was destroyed upon re-entering the Earth's atmosphere like a meteor. By this point, Sputnik had spent a total of 92 days in space. This was a tremendous achievement for science, and marked the dawn for SPACE TRAVEL!

First Animal In Space

One of the first inhabitants of Earth to conquer space was a small dog named LAIKA. She was the first animal to orbit around Earth in 1957.

First Man On The Moon

The AMERICANS eventually caught up with the Soviet Union and managed to send a team of three astronauts to the Moon for the first time in 1969, just twelve years after Sputnik.

Space Race

The success of Sputnik took the world by surprise, and sparked a space race between the UNITED STATES OF AMERICA and the SOVIET UNION.

First Cosmonaut

YURI GAGARIN, a Soviet cosmonaut, was the first human in space. He spent almost two hours in space in 1961 before returning safely.

Space Travel Today

Space travel has become a fairly normal thing since those pioneering days. Rockets are sent to space quite often, carrying satellites for various purposes, from science to communication. They often take supplies to the INTERNATIONAL SPACE STATION — home to astronauts since the year 2000.

Unmanned Space Exploration

The Moon is the furthest-away object from Earth that humans have stepped foot on... so far!

All the missions to visit other planets like Mars, or asteroids, or even explorations of the edges of our Solar System, have been done by space probes. It would be far too dangerous to send humans to these places before we know more about them, and, on top of that, it takes a tremendous amount more technical effort to send a human rather than a space probe.

Space probes are computers, or sometimes robots, that do not need oxygen or food, and they do not need to come home to Earth after they have completed their mission.

Mission to Mars

The early space probes were complicated CAMERAS with a few additional sensors, but as technology progressed, more advanced space probes could be made.

In 1996, NASA sent the first robot to Mars in a mission named 'Mars Pathfinder'. The space probe consisted of a landing unit with tools to measure the weather and the temperature and cameras.

Also on board this mission was a small 10-kilogram robot named Sojourner, which was able to drive around on Mars' surface. Sojourner was able to collect fifteen soil and rock samples from Mars and analyse them.

It was a big success and the United States have launched two similar, but bigger missions to explore Mars since: Spirit and Opportunity in 2004.

Lunar Mission

Before humans set foot on the Moon, a series of space probes, the Lunar and Ranger Missions, EXPLORED THE MOON and took pictures of its surface from close range.

Rosetta Mission

There have also been missions to explore smaller objects, like comets. The Rosetta mission, which consisted of a PROBE and a small attached spacecraft robot named PHILAE, was rocket-launched in 2004.

Rosetta passed Mars and two asteroids, and it detached Philae in 2014. Philae headed for a nearby COMET and managed to safely land on its surface to analyse the material the comet was made of.

Voyager 1

So far, most space exploration has been about our own Solar System, but there are some space probes that have travelled MUCH FURTHER.

The space probe furthest from Earth is Voyager 1, which left 36 years ago. On its journey it passed JUPITER and SATURN to take pictures of these planets and their Moons...

...And it has now reached the EDGE OF OUR SOLAR SYSTEM to explore the space beyond. It has travelled further than anyone — or anything! — in history.

Life On Other Planets

Are we alone in the universe? Is there another civilization on a different planet that could communicate with us?

We haven't been contacted by any alien species so far... At least we haven't discovered a message! But there are millions and millions of other Solar Systems in our own galaxy, the Milky Way, let alone the whole universe, and it does not seem impossible that the conditions for the existence of another habitable planet might exist elsewhere.

Habitable Planets

The conditions for life to come into existence need to be PERFECTLY BALANCED — life can't exist on just any old planet (for instance, life is not possible on our two neighbouring planets, Venus and Mars).

Earth's orbit lies in the HABITABLE ZONE of our Solar System: it is far away enough for the Sun not to evaporate all water, but it is close enough for the Sun to provide enough heat to keep the water on Earth's surface liquid.

WATER is the foundation of life as we know it — without water, scientists don't think life is possible.

Recently, astronomers have discovered thousands of DISTANT SOLAR SYSTEMS with a planet a similar size to Earth, inside the so-called habitable zone.

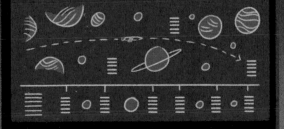

Search For Life

Scientists search for life outside of Earth, (so-called extra-terrestrial life) mostly through analysing RADIO WAVES from space to seek out messages from other planets.

Message into the Unknown

Some of the space probes we've sent from Earth have carried MESSAGES to other life forms in the unlikely case that they might find the probe some day. But how would we communicate with another species? We certainly wouldn't speak the same language.

Voyager 1 carried a GOLDEN RECORD, which should be playable for the next 500 million years. On the golden cover are instructions on how to play and decode the record, and how to find our Solar System. It contains more than one hundred pictures and sounds from our Solar System, Earth, science, sports, education, and information about us humans.

The Golden Record

First published in Great Britain in 2016 by Wide Eyed Editions,
an imprint of Aurum Press, 74–77 White Lion Street, London N1 9PF
QuartoKnows.com
Visit our blogs at QuartoKnows.com

Destination: Space copyright © Aurum Press Ltd 2016
Illustrations copyright © Tom Clohosy Cole 2016
Written by Dr Christoph Englert

All rights reserved

No part of this publication may be reproduced, stored in a retrieval system, or transmitted,
in any form, or by any means, electrical, mechanical, photocopying, recording or otherwise
without the prior written permission of the publisher or a licence permitting restricted copying.
In the United Kingdom such licences are issued by the Copyright Licensing Agency,
Barnard's Inn, 86 Fetter Lane, London EC4A 1EN.

A catalogue record for this book is available from the British Library.

ISBN 978-1-84780-824-0

The illustrations were created digitally
Set in Trio Grotesk, Turnip and Playtime With Hot Toddy

Designed by Joe Hales
Edited by Jenny Broom
Published by Rachel Williams
Production by Jenny Cundill

Printed in China

1 3 5 7 9 8 6 4 2

FSC
www.fsc.org
MIX
Paper from
responsible sources
FSC® C104723